STAMPABILITY

VINEYARD

STEWART & SALLY WALTON

PHOTOGRAPHY BY GRAHAM RAE

LORENZ BOOKS

LONDON • NEW YORK • SYDNEY • BATH

CONTENTS

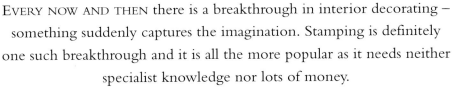

$\mathcal{I}$NTRODUCTION

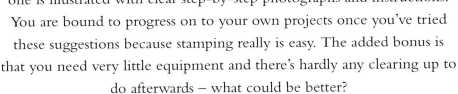

EVERY NOW AND THEN there is a breakthrough in interior decorating –
something suddenly captures the imagination. Stamping is definitely
one such breakthrough and it is all the more popular as it needs neither
specialist knowledge nor lots of money.

All you need is a stamp and some colour and you can make a start. The
idea comes from the office rubber stamp and it uses the same principle.
You can use stamps with a stamp pad, but a small foam roller gives a
better effect. The stamp can be coated with ordinary household paint –
this makes stamping a fairly inexpensive option, and gives you a wide
range of colours to choose from.

There are stamping projects in this book ranging from personalizing a
set of stationery, an old wooden wine crate or picture frame to giving
your bedroom, kitchen or hallway a fresh, new co-ordinated look. Each
one is illustrated with clear step-by-step photographs and instructions.
You are bound to progress on to your own projects once you've tried
these suggestions because stamping really is easy. The added bonus is
that you need very little equipment and there's hardly any clearing up to
do afterwards – what could be better?

This book features the vineyard, comprising a bunch of grapes, a leaf
and a tendril stamp. Each of these can be used alone on smaller items or
in combination with the others to make a trailing grapevine frieze.
People have decorated their homes with painted, carved and printed
vines since classical times, making this one of the most enduring
decorating motifs of all.

The inspirational powers of the grapevine are unsurpassed – luscious
bunches of swollen fruit, shapely green leaves and twirling tendrils –
and if that isn't enough, just think of the wine! What better way to
appreciate the vine's graceful lines – first decorate, then celebrate!

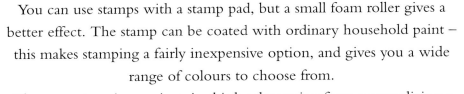
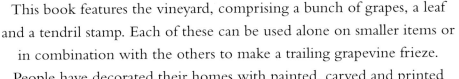
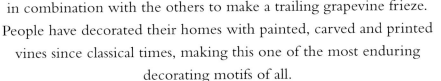
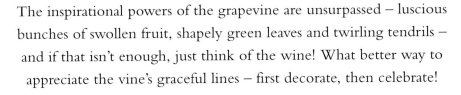

BASIC APPLICATION TECHNIQUES

Stamping is a simple and direct way of making a print. The variations, such as they are, come from the way in which the stamp is inked and the type of surface to which it is applied. The stamps used in the projects were inked with a foam roller which is easy to do and gives reliable results, but each application technique has its own character. It is a good idea to experiment and find the method and effect that you most prefer.

INKING WITH A BRUSH

The advantage of this technique is that you can see where the colour has been applied. This method is quite time-consuming, so use it for smaller projects. It is ideal for inking an intricate stamp with more than one colour.

INKING WITH A FOAM ROLLER

This is the best method for stamping large areas, such as walls. The stamp is evenly inked and you can see where the colour has been applied. Variations in the strength of printing can be achieved by only re-inking the stamp after several printings.

INKING ON A STAMP PAD

This is the traditional way to ink rubber stamps, which are less porous than foam stamps. The method suits small projects, particularly those involving printing on paper. Stamp pads are more expensive to use than paint but are less messy, and will produce very crisp prints.

INKING BY DIPPING IN PAINT

Spread a thin layer of paint on to a flat plate and dip the stamp into it. This is the quickest way of stamping large decorating projects. As you cannot see how much paint the stamp is picking up, you will need to experiment.

INKING WITH FABRIC PAINT

Spread a thin layer of fabric paint on to a flat plate and dip the stamp into it. Fabric paints are quite sticky and any excess paint is likely to be taken up in the fabric rather than to spread around the edges. Fabric paint can also be applied by brush or foam roller, and is available with integral applicators from specialist outlets.

INKING WITH SEVERAL COLOURS

A brush is the preferred option when using more than one colour on a stamp. It allows greater accuracy than a foam roller because you can see exactly where you are putting the colour. Two-colour stamping is very effective for giving a shadow effect or a decorative pattern.

SURFACE APPLICATIONS

The surface on to which you stamp your design will greatly influence the finished effect.
Below are just some of the effects which can be achieved.

STAMPING ON ROUGH PLASTER
You can roughen your walls before stamping by mixing filler to a fairly loose consistency and spreading it randomly on the wall. When dry, roughen with coarse sandpaper, using random strokes.

STAMPING ON SMOOTH PLASTER OR LINING PAPER
Ink the stamp with a small foam roller for the crispest print. You can create perfect repeats by re-inking with every print, whereas making several prints between inkings varies the strength of the prints and is more in keeping with hand-printing.

STAMPING ON WOOD
Rub down the surface of any wood to give the paint a better "key" to adhere to. Some woods are very porous and absorb paint, but you can intensify the colour by over-printing later. Wood looks best lightly stamped so that the grain shows through. Seal your design with clear matt varnish.

STAMPING ON GLASS
Wash glass in hot water and detergent to remove any dirt or grease and dry thoroughly. It is best to stamp on glass for non-food uses, such as vases or sun-catchers. Ink the stamp with a foam roller and practise on a spare sheet of glass. As glass has a slippery, non-porous surface, you need to apply the stamp with a direct on/off movement. Each print will have a slightly different character, and the glass's transparency allows the pattern to be viewed from all sides.

STAMPING ON TILES
Wash and dry glazed tiles thoroughly before stamping. If the tiles are already on the wall, avoid stamping in areas which require a lot of cleaning. The paint will only withstand a gentle wipe with a damp cloth. Loose tiles can be baked to add strength and permanence to the paint. Read the paint manufacturer's instructions (and disclaimers!) before you do this. Ink the stamp with a small foam roller and apply with a direct on/off movement.

STAMPING ON FABRIC
As a rule, natural fabrics are the most absorbent, but to judge the stamped effect, experiment on a small sample. Fabric paints come in a range of colours, but to obtain the subtler shades you may need to combine the primaries and black and white. Always place a sheet of card behind the fabric to protect your work surface. Apply the fabric paint with a foam roller, brush or by dipping. You will need more paint than for a wall, as fabric absorbs the paint more efficiently.

Paint Effects

Once you have mastered the basics of stamp decorating, there are other techniques that you can use to enrich the patterns and add variety. Stamped patterns can be glazed over, rubbed back or over-printed to inject subtle or dramatic character changes.

STAMPING EMULSION ON PLASTER, DISTRESSED WITH TINTED VARNISH

The stamped pattern will already have picked up the irregularities of the wall surface and, if you re-ink after several prints, some prints will look more faded than others. To give the appearance of old hand-blocked wallpaper, paint over the whole surface with a ready-mixed antiquing varnish. You can also add colour to a varnish, but never mix a water-based product with a spirit-based one.

STAMPING EMULSION ON PLASTER, COLOURED WITH TINTED VARNISH

If the stamped prints have dried to a brighter or duller shade than you had hoped for, you can apply a coat of coloured varnish. It is possible to buy ready-mixed colour-tinted varnish or you can add colour to a clear varnish base. A blue tint will change a red into purple, a red will change yellow into orange, and so on. The colour changes are gentle because the background changes at the same time.

STAMPING WITH WALLPAPER PASTE, PVA GLUE AND WATERCOLOUR PAINT

Mix three parts pre-mixed wallpaper paste with one part PVA glue and add watercolours. These come ready-mixed in bottles with integral droppers. The colours are intense so you many only need a few drops. The combination gives a sticky substance which the stamp picks up well and which clings to the wall without drips. The PVA glue dries clear to give a bright, glazed finish.

STAMPING WITH A MIXTURE OF WALLPAPER PASTE AND EMULSION

Mix up some wallpaper paste and add one part to two parts emulsion. This mixture makes a thicker print that is less opaque than the usual emulsion version. It also has a glazed surface that picks up the light.

STAMPING EMULSION ON PLASTER, WITH A SHADOW EFFECT

Applying even pressure gives a flat, regular print. By pressing down more firmly on one side of the stamp you can create a shadow effect on one edge. This is most effective if you repeat the procedure, placing the emphasis on the same side each time.

STAMPING A DROPPED SHADOW EFFECT

To make a pattern appear three-dimensional, stamp each pattern twice. Make the first print in a dark colour that shows up well against a mid-tone background. For the second print, move the stamp slightly to one side and use a lighter colour.

DESIGNING WITH STAMPS

To design the pattern of stamps, you need to find a compromise between printing totally at random and measuring precisely to achieve a machine-printed regularity. To do this, you can use the stamp block itself to give you a means of measuring your pattern, or try strips of paper, squares of card and lengths of string. Try using a stamp pad on scrap paper to plan your design but always wash and dry the stamp before proceeding to the main event.

USING PAPER CUT-OUTS
The easiest way to plan your design is to stamp and cut out as many pattern elements as you need and use them to mark the position of your finished stamped prints.

CREATING A REPEAT PATTERN
Use a strip of paper as a measuring device for repeat patterns. Cut the strip the length of one row of the pattern. Use the stamp block to mark where each print will go, with equal spaces in between. You could also mark up a vertical strip. Position the horizontal strip against this to print.

USING A PAPER SPACING DEVICE
This method is very simple. Decide on the distance between prints and cut a strip of paper to that size. Each time you stamp, place the strip against the edge of the previous print and line up the edge of the block with the other side of the strip. Use a longer strip to measure the distance required.

CREATING AN IRREGULAR PATTERN
If your design doesn't fit into a regular grid, plan the pattern first on paper. Cut out paper shapes to represent the spaces and use these to position the finished pattern. Alternatively, raise a motif above the previous one by stamping above a strip of card positioned on the baseline.

DEVISING A LARGER MOTIF
Use the stamps in groups to make up a larger design. Try stamping four together in a block, or partially overlapping an edge so that only a section of the stamp is shown. Use the stamps upside down, back to back and rotated in different ways. Experiment on scrap paper first.

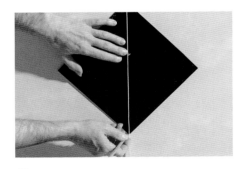

USING A PLUMBLINE
Attach a plumbline at ceiling height to hang down the wall. Hold a card square behind the plumbline so that the string cuts through two opposite corners. Mark all four points, then move the card square down. Continue in this way to make a grid for stamping a regular pattern.

GRAPE JUG

A white ceramic jug like this one seems to be crying out for some stamped decoration, and the grapevine stamps do the trick in minutes. Choose a well-proportioned plain jug and transform it into something that is decorative as well as practical. Acrylic enamel paint is new on the market and, although it resembles ordinary enamel, it is in fact water-based and does not require harmful solvents for cleaning brushes and stamps. Follow the manufacturer's instructions to "fire" the stamped jug in a domestic oven to add strength and permanence to the pattern. Without "firing", the paint will only stand up to non-abrasive cleaning.

YOU WILL NEED
white ceramic jug
clean cloth
grape, tendril and leaf stamps
black stamp pad
scrap paper
scissors
acrylic enamel paint in black and
ultramarine blue
plate
foam roller

1 Wash the jug in hot water and detergent, then wipe dry to ensure that there is no grease on the surface.

2 Print a grape, a tendril and a leaf on to scrap paper and cut them out. Arrange them on the jug to plan the finished design.

3 Mix together the black and the blue acrylic enamel paint on a plate. Run the roller through the paint until it is evenly coated and ink the stamps. Stamp the motifs following your planned arrangement as a guide.

4 The leaf may be used to fill any gaps, or the pattern may be repeated on the other side. Follow the manufacturer's instructions if you wish to make the design permanent by "firing" in the oven.

COUNTRY KITCHEN

Specialist suppliers sell beautifully decorated tiles but they can be very expensive. So why not use stamps and paint to make your own set of exclusive tiles? The grape stamp is inked with two shades of green that blend in the middle in a slightly different way each time. Small touches such as the rustic hanging rail and the wooden plate add rustic authenticity to a country kitchen. The wood for the rail needs to be old and weathered. The nails banged into the rail as hangers are called "cut" nails, which are used for floorboarding. Attach the rail to the wall and hang fresh herbs from it, conveniently close to the cooker. The wooden plate is stamped with different parts of the tendril motif to make a decorative border and central design.

YOU WILL NEED
plain tiles
clean cloths
acrylic enamel paint in blue-green and
yellow-green
plates
foam rollers
grape, leaf and tendril stamps
olive-green emulsion or acrylic paint
scrap paper
weathered piece of wood, maximum
30cm/12in long
long cut nails or hooks
hammer or drill
black stamp pad
scissors
wooden plate, sanded to remove any
stain or varnish
vegetable oil

1 Wash the tiles in hot water and detergent, then wipe dry to ensure that there is no grease on the surface.

2 Spread some blue-green acrylic enamel paint on to one plate and some yellow-green on to another. Run the rollers through the paint until they are evenly coated.

3 Ink the leaf, the top and the right side of the grape stamp with the blue-green roller. Ink the rest of the stamp with the yellow-green roller.

4 Stamp a bunch of grapes in the centre of each tile. Remove the stamp directly, taking care not to smudge the print. If you do make a mistake, wipe off the paint with a clean cloth and start again. Follow the manufacturer's instructions to "fire" the tiles in the oven if required.

5 For the hanging rail, spread some olive-green emulsion paint on to a plate and run the roller through it until it is evenly coated. Ink the leaf stamp and stamp twice on to scrap paper to remove some of the paint.

6 Stamp on to the length of weathered wood without re-inking the stamp. The resulting print will be light and faded-looking, like the wood itself. Make as many prints as you can fit along the length. Hammer in the nails or drill and screw in the hooks to complete the hanging rail.

7 For the wooden plate, stamp several tendrils on to scrap paper and cut them out. Arrange them on the plate to work out the spacing and positioning of the motifs.

8 Spread some olive-green emulsion or acrylic paint on to a plate and run the roller through it until it is evenly coated. Ink the corner of the tendril stamp comprising the two curls that will make up the border pattern and carefully begin stamping around the edge of the plate.

9 Ink the whole stamp and stamp two tendrils in the centre of the plate. Leave to dry.

10 Dip a clean cloth into some vegetable oil and rub this into the whole surface of the plate, including the stamped pattern. You can repeat this process once all the oil has been absorbed into the wood. Each time you rub oil into the plate, the colour of the wood will deepen.

WOODEN WINE CRATE

Old wood usually looks best with a faded rather than freshly painted pattern. The grape design here does not detract from the crate's rustic quality because it has been stamped in a muted green, then rubbed back to blend with the existing lettering on the wood. If you are lucky enough to find a custom-made wine crate like this one, it will simply need a good scrubbing with soapy water, then be left to dry before you stamp it.

YOU WILL NEED
old wine crate or similar wooden box
scrubbing brush (optional)
olive-green emulsion paint
plate
foam roller
grape stamp
fine sandpaper

1 If necessary, scrub the crate well with soapy water and a scrubbing brush and leave it to dry.

2 Spread some olive-green emulsion paint on to a plate and run the roller through it until it is evenly coated. Ink the stamp and begin stamping a random pattern of grapes. Stamp at different angles to add variety.

3 Cover all the surfaces of the crate, overlapping the edge if the planks are too narrow to take the whole motif.

4 Leave the paint to dry, then rub back the pattern with sandpaper, so that it becomes faded and blends with the original surface decoration or lettering. Rub gently and aim for a patchy, distressed appearance.

$\mathcal{T}$USCAN HALLWAY

All three stamps are used in this project to transform a dull space into a wall frieze that you will want to preserve forever. The finished wall will bring a touch of Tuscany into your home, even when the sky is a gloomy grey outside. The wall is divided at dado height with a strong burgundy red below and a warm cream above to visually lower the ceiling. The vine leaf pattern has been stamped on to a grid of pencil marks that is simple to measure out using a square of card and a plumbline. The lines are hand-painted using a wooden batten as a hand rest but you could also stick parallel strips of masking tape around the walls and fill in the stripes between.

YOU WILL NEED
tape measure
pencil
ruler
emulsion paint in cream, burgundy,
terracotta, white and black
large household paintbrush
wallpaper paste, mixed according to the
manufacturer's instructions
plate
foam roller
grape, leaf and tendril stamps
thin strip of card
long-bristled lining brush
straight-edged wooden batten, 1m/1yd
long
plumbline
15 x 15cm/6 x 6in card
square-tipped artist's paintbrush
clear gloss, matt or satin varnish
and brush

1 Measure the height of a dado rail and draw a line around the wall with a ruler and pencil. Paint the wall above the line cream and the area below burgundy. Mix roughly equal amounts of wallpaper paste, burgundy and terracotta paint on a plate.

2 Run the roller through the mixture until it is evenly coated and ink the grape stamp. Align the strip of card with the top of the burgundy section. Rest the base of the stamp block on the card to stamp a row of grapes.

3 Ink the tendril stamp and stamp a tendril at the top of each bunch of grapes. Allow some prints to be paler than others as the paint wears off the stamp block, to give a faded and patchy effect.

4 Mix a little cream paint into some white. With the lining brush, apply highlights to the grapes and the tendrils. Let the brushstrokes vary in direction and weight to add to the hand-painted look. Support your painting hand with your free hand.

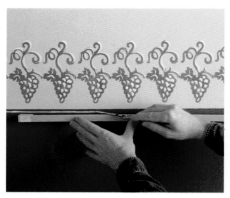

5 Hold the batten just below the top edge of the burgundy section and rest your painting hand on it. Slide your hand along the batten to paint a smooth, thin line in off-white. Practise this movement first and try to relax your hand to avoid jerky lines. A slight waviness to the line will not spoil the effect. Try to avoid having to paint over the line, as a single, fresh brushstroke looks better.

6 Attach a plumbline above dado height, just in from one corner and so that it hangs down to the skirting board. Place the card square against the wall so that the string cuts through the top and bottom corners. Mark all the corner points in pencil.

7 Move the card down so that the top corner rests on the lowest pencil mark. Complete one column of the grid in this way, then move the plumbline across and continue until the lower wall is completely covered with a grid of pencil marks.

8 Mix a small amount of black paint into the burgundy to deepen the colour. Spread some dark burgundy paint on to a plate and run the roller through it until it is evenly coated. Ink the leaf stamp and make a print on one of the pencil marks.

9 Position the stamp just above or just below the pencil mark each time to create a regular pattern over the whole lower wall.

10 Move the batten about 2.5cm/ 1in from the cream dado line and use the square-tipped artist's brush to paint a second, broader line. Keep the line as fresh as possible; visible brushstrokes are preferable to solid, flat colour. Apply a coat of varnish to the lower wall to seal and protect the paint.

VINE LEAF CUTLERY RACK

A small wooden cutlery rack like this one provides another ideal surface for stamping. Use the stamps to loosely co-ordinate your kitchen or dining room without being swamped by matching patterns and colours. The wood has been stained blue and is then rubbed back to reveal some of the natural grain underneath. The two colours of the pattern are stamped separately using thinned emulsion for a light and airy finish.

YOU WILL NEED
wooden cutlery rack, stained blue
fine sandpaper
emulsion or acrylic paint in dark and light
olive-green
plate
foam roller
leaf stamp

1 Sand the surface of the cutlery rack to reveal some of the grain. Spread some dark olive-green paint on to a plate and thin it with water to a runny consistency.

2 Use the roller to ink the leaf stamp. Print two leaves side by side on the back and front of the rack and two leaves one above the other on the sides. Leave to dry.

3 Spread some light olive-green paint on to a plate and run the roller through it until it is evenly coated. Ink just the tips of the leaves and overprint all the darker green prints. If some of the prints are slightly off-register, this will only add to the rustic appearance of the rack.

TABLE NAPKINS

These stamped table napkins look great with rush mats on a wooden table top. They bring together even the most casual collection of plates, glasses and cutlery to look like a deliberate choice. You can buy a set of plain table napkins or make your own by sewing straight seams along the edges of squares of cotton fabric. Stamping on fabric is easy and special fabric paints can be heat-treated with a hot iron to make the pattern permanent. Follow the manufacturer's instructions, which may vary from brand to brand.

YOU WILL NEED
terracotta-coloured table napkins
iron
newspaper
cream-coloured fabric paint
plate
foam roller
grape and tendril stamps

2 Stamp a bunch of grapes halfway along each edge, then ink the tendril stamp and print tendrils between the grapes. Stamp all the napkins in this way and leave to dry. Seal the design with an iron, following the paint manufacturer's instructions.

1 Wash and iron the napkins to remove any glaze which may block the paint's absorption. Lay the first napkin on top of several sheets of newspaper. Spread some cream fabric paint on to a plate and run the roller through it until it is evenly coated. Ink the grape stamp and print a bunch of grapes in each corner of the napkin.

VINTAGE GLASS BOWL

Turn a plain glass bowl into an exquisite table centrepiece by stamping a white tendril pattern on the outside. Stamped glassware looks wonderful because the opaque patterns seem to intermingle as you look through the transparent glass. Another advantage is that you can see the stamp as the print is being made, which helps you to position it correctly and avoid overlaps and smudges. Glass painting has become popular recently and there are several brands of specialist glass paint available. Acrylic enamel paint has a good consistency for stamping and is water-based, allowing you to simply wipe it off and start again if you make a mistake.

YOU WILL NEED
plain glass bowl
clean cloth
white acrylic enamel paint
plate
foam roller
tendril stamp

1 Wash the bowl in hot water and detergent, then wipe dry to ensure that there is no grease on the surface. Spread some white acrylic enamel paint on to a plate and run the roller through it until it is evenly coated.

2 Ink the tendril stamp and stamp the first row of prints around the base of the bowl. Remove the stamp directly, taking care that it does not slide or smudge the print. If you do make a mistake, wipe off the paint with a clean cloth and start again.

3 Turn the stamp the other way up to stamp the second row, positioning the prints in between the tendrils on the first row, so that there are no obvious gaps.

4 Stamp one more row with the stamp the original way up. Allow the stamp to overlap the edge of the bowl, so that most of the stem is left out. Leave the bowl to dry or "fire" it in the oven to fix the design, following the paint manufacturer's instructions.

STATIONERY, NOTEBOOKS AND FOLDERS

Have fun experimenting with stamp designs and create your own range of stationery at the same time. The stamps can be used alone or in combination with each other to make a whole range of patterns linked by the use of colour to form a set. Here, the plain books, folders and stationery are all a natural brown and the pattern is stamped in a sepia tone, which complements the colour of the paper. Mixing extender or PVA glue into the paint will make the paint dry more slowly, giving you extra time to work. Hand-printed stationery is very quick and easy to make and will give great pleasure as an individual gift.

YOU WILL NEED
sepia-coloured acrylic paint and extender or
PVA glue
plates
foam rollers
grape, tendril and leaf stamps
scrap paper
notebooks
brown parcel wrap
scalpel or craft knife
cutting mat
off-white acrylic or emulsion paint
folder
paintbrush
small file
handmade paper folded into cards
natural brown envelopes

1 Spread some sepia paint on to a plate. Add extender or PVA glue and mix together.

2 Run a roller through the paint until it is evenly coated and ink the grape stamp. Make several test prints on scrap paper to gauge the way the paper absorbs the paint and how much paint you will need to apply to the stamp to achieve the desired effect.

3 Stamp a bunch of grapes in the middle of a notebook cover.

4 Ink the tendril stamp and surround the grapes with tendril motifs. The pattern can be repeated on the back cover of the notebook.

5 Stamp a bunch of grapes on to a small piece of brown parcel wrap. Carefully cut around the outline with a scalpel or craft knife on a cutting mat to make a stencil.

6 Spread some off-white paint on to a plate and run a roller through it until it is evenly coated. Position the stencil on a notebook cover and run the roller over the stencil to make a solid grape shape. Leave to dry.

7 Ink the grape stamp with sepia and over-print the stencilled shape to add the detail.

8 Cut a window from a sheet of scrap paper the same size as the folder cover to make a paper frame.

9 Lay the frame on the cover. Ink the leaf stamp with sepia and stamp leaves all over the cover, overlapping the frame. Leave to dry, then remove the paper frame to reveal a plain border around the leaf pattern.

10 Mix some off-white paint into the sepia to make a lighter brown. Using a brush, apply the lighter brown paint to one side of the grape stamp and sepia to the other.

11 Stamp one bunch of grapes on to the cover of a small file. The shape will be shaded on one side, creating a three-dimensional effect.

12 Place the folded cards of handmade paper on sheets of scrap paper. Stamp an all-over pattern of sepia tendrils, overlapping the edges so that the cards look as if they have been cut from a larger sheet of stamped paper. The texture of the paper will show through in places and the colour will vary as the paint gradually wears off the stamp, adding to the rich, handmade effect.

PICTURE FRAME

A decorated frame draws attention to the picture within, while providing another opportunity to add colour and pattern to a room. This frame can be hung with the broad end at either the top or the bottom depending on the nature of the picture it surrounds. The balance of the grape, leaf and tendril motif is reinforced by using the same colours to paint the border lines. Practise using a long-bristled lining brush on paper first before you paint the fine lines on the frame. The "hands on" style does not require perfection – slightly wavy lines add character.

YOU WILL NEED
grape, leaf and tendril stamps
black stamp pad
scrap paper
scissors
picture frame, painted brick-red with an
olive-green border
set square
pencil
emulsion or acrylic paint in olive-green and
ultramarine blue
plate
foam roller
long-bristled lining brush
damp cloth (optional)

1 Stamp all three motifs on to scrap paper and cut them out. Position them on the frame to plan your design.

2 Use a set square and pencil to draw a line around the frame, just inside the green border. Draw a second line around the centre of the frame.

3 Spread some olive-green paint on to one side of the plate and blue on to the other. Run the roller through the paint until it is evenly coated, allowing the colours to blend slightly in the middle. Ink the stamps and print the motifs in the planned positions.

4 Use the lining brush to paint the pencil lines ultramarine blue. Steady your hand by sliding it along the raised border as you work. If you make a very obvious mistake, wipe off the paint immediately with a damp cloth, but you may need to touch up the background colour when the new line has dried.

Beautiful Bedroom

Who wouldn't want to sleep in this lavender-grey and white bedroom? The choice of two cool colours has a very calming effect. The frieze is stamped in white at dado height around a lavender-grey wall. The simple reversal of the wall colours on the headboard provides both contrast and continuity. You can stamp on to an existing headboard or make one quite simply from a sheet of MDF cut to the width of the bed. Use the stamps to make matching accessories in the same colours. Make the most of the stamps' versatility by using only the central part of the tendril stamp on the narrow border of a picture frame.

You will need
drawing pin
string
spirit level
emulsion paint in white and lavender-grey
plates
foam rollers
tendril, grape and leaf stamps
headboard or sheet of MDF painted white
masking tape
pencil
ruler
broad, square-tipped artist's paintbrush

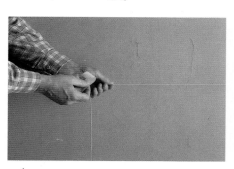

1 Use a drawing pin to attach one end of the string in a corner of the room at dado height. Run the string along the wall to the next corner and secure the end. Check the string with a spirit level and adjust if necessary.

2 Spread some white emulsion paint on to a plate and run a roller through it until it is evenly coated. Ink all three stamps and stamp a tendril, grape and leaf in sequence along the wall. Align the top edge of each stamp with the string and print below it.

3 When the first wall is complete, move the string to the next wall and continue all the way around the room. To decorate the headboard, stick masking tape around the top and side edges of the white board.

4 Spread some lavender-grey paint on to a plate and run a roller through it until it is evenly coated. Ink the leaf and tendril stamps. Align the stamp block with the masking tape and stamp alternate leaves and tendrils down both sides of the board.

5 Ink all three stamps and stamp a tendril, grape and leaf along the top edge of the board. Repeat the sequence to complete the row. Check the spacing before you stamp – wide spacing is better than the motifs appearing squashed together.

6 Measure a central panel on the board and lightly draw it in pencil. Stick strips of masking tape around the panel and the border. Mix some lavender-grey and white paint, then paint the border and the central panel in this pale grey colour.

First published in 1996 by Lorenz Books

Lorenz Books is an imprint of Anness Publishing Limited
Boundary Row Studios
1 Boundary Row
London SE1 8HP

ISBN 1 85967 233 7

Distributed in Canada by Raincoast Books Distribution Limited

A CIP catalogue record for this book is available from the British Library

Publisher: Joanna Lorenz
Project Editor: Lindsay Porter
Designer: Bobbie Colgate Stone
Photographer: Graham Rae
Stylist: Andrea Spencer

Printed and bound in Singapore

ACKNOWLEDGMENTS
The authors and publishers would like to thank Sacha Cohen, Josh George and Sarah Pullin for all their hard work in the studio.

Paints supplied by
Crown Paints, Crown Decorative Products Ltd, PO Box 37, Crown House, Hollins Road, Darwen, Lancashire.

Specialist paints supplied by Paint Magic, 79 Shepperton Road, Islington, London.